Next Level

Voice Over Domination

By Earl Hall

ISBN: 9781720174066
Imprint: Independently published

PREFACE

This book is the only book showing actual steps to becoming a voice-over artist from ground zero. More than that it will give you the mindset you actually need to have to build an actual voice over business. Let's just be real. You can find these tactics and strategies anywhere. Well some of them anyway. Most books like this never give you the actual **'thing'** that is going to set you on the path to discovering your actual purpose in this thing called voice over. this book will.

With this book you will learn how to setup your home studio (this is the future of voice-over by the way), how to use your DAW, and most importantly, how to build your career in voice-over. In a nutshell. Your most important job as a voice-over is to get clients!

Since 2008 I have purchased books and courses online, with the promise of 6 figure incomes and all while working from home in voice-over. What I never was able to discover after all that money spent was **what actually works**. What is the strategy? What is the secret sauce? What is the secret to making an income from home in voice-over?

I have gotten some good information from the known voice-over coaches out there. But nothing has ever been put down on paper like what I am about to do here. This book is actionable. You can use this as a guide and start executing and building your voice-over career. Not only do you have access to this book. You also have access to several training videos that you can access right now and implement into your business to jump start it.

I am going to give you the facts about becoming a voice-over artist. I am going to show you how to start, build, and grow a successful voice-over business.

Have the #GrindAndDontQuit mentality & the understanding NEVER WAIT FOR PERMISSION FROM ANYONE TO BE GREAT & you will win.

Introduction

In 2004 I began my fascination with being on the microphone. I began my first internet radio station. At the time I was using a headset mic. But mostly the station just played gospel music. I went on live from time to time. I realize now that the LIVE part was what got my juices going. By 2006 I was podcasting and by 2008 I was doing it big (at least I thought so).
I actually had developed my own radio studio in my basement and was broadcasting live to the world. I had on air guests. Took live calls. The whole 9.

I signed up for the two big P2P sites and thought I was about to get rich. I mean I had my Electrovoice RE20, my Heil PR40, my big as mixer, a DBX 286a (don't make those any more), and 2 computers. I was about to blow up.

I'm sure I don't have to tell you that that didn't happen.
I was doing auditions. I was reaching out to business. I was buying all the stuff the industry was telling me I needed.

Yet I was making NO MONEY!

During this same time I was coming out of a 5 year depression after the failure of my first business. I was the COO and one of the owners of an engineering design firm. We served big names like Harley Davidson, Oshkosh Truck, Kraft Foods, and major firms across the country. Some folks in Tennessee, Belgium, and India where interested in what I was doing and wanted to partner with me to take this global. Well the biggest lesson I learned here was, never take money from anyone. He who controls the money controls the business.

Long story short. Those money people, against my advice, brought in partners that killed what I had built.

After about 5 years of depression and self hate. I woke up and dived head first into my real love...VOICE-OVER.

After all of that. I started to figure this thing out. I started doing the thing that we all need to do. I started studying MARKETING. Not marketing from the voice-over perspective. I studied top internet marketers. Like Simon Sinek, Jay Abraham, Russell Brunson, and many others. In the world we live in, knowing and understanding internet marketing is vital.

Understanding how to utilize email marketing, social media marketing, and the freelance sites is what is going to make the difference. Knowing how to do voice-over and mastering your DAW is only about 30% of the equation. The rest is marketing.

I will never forget the moment. The moment I went from satisfied to terrified. I was laying on the ground. Soft grass under me as I looked up at the sun between the trees and leaves blowing in the cool breeze. It was in Sherman park, on the northern side of Milwaukee. It was in the "hood" but it was peaceful.

I was a bus operator waiting for my shift to start on the route 30. I was completely satisfied. I figured that I would retire from this job and live my life out in this city. My bus pulled up and I saw the bus operator I was to relieve. In that moment, I realized that this is not how I am wired. This is not who I am.

In an instant I realized I wanted more. I needed more. I was not satisfied and would never be in this job. During my shift I plotted and planned what I would do to make sure I lived the life I wanted to live. On my terms, no one else's. I had to build the life I wanted for me. Not my family, but just for me.

Even though that may sound completely selfish. Well, it is. It's kinda like the instructions on the airplane. You know. Put your oxygen max on first, then help others. It's like that.

I knew I had to build my own business. It was going to take hard work and sacrifice. The first thing I did was take a huge pay cut by leaving driving and going to work in the garage. I did this to be able to have a regular schedule. As a bus operator in Milwaukee there is just no way to work a straight 8 hour day.

Well my new schedule for almost 3 years was this...
Start work at 7pm
Off at 3:30am
Sleep from 4am to 7am
Take kids to school
Build business 8am to noon
Take a nap from noon to 2pm
Pick kids up from school
Nap from 4pm to 6pm
7pm Work

Of course some days I missed a nap here and there because of work coming in to my business. But it did not matter. I wanted this and I was willing to work for it.

I ignored all the people that said I couldn't do this. I shut out all the naysayers, doubters, and haters. On November 17, 2017, I punched out for the last time and have been building the business of my dreams ever since.

On my 3 year journey, I had made a firm decision that I was going to live life on my own terms. I was going to do this. Failure was not an option. I never allowed an excuse to grow in my mind. Sure, self-doubt would creep in sometimes. I just never let it take hold. I knew beyond a shadow of a doubt that success or failure was completely in my hands.

There would be no excuses.

I know that you may be dealing with uncertain situations right now. Situations that will seemingly force you down a path you don't want to go. I want to encourage you to take the path YOU want to take. Not the easy one. Not the one that life seems to pushing you towards.

Take control and know your success is completely up to you. I want to invite you to share in my journey. I am living my dream of being self-employed and living life on my own terms. I want to show you how to do it too.

Are you willing to sacrifice for your own success? Are you willing to go harder and then anyone else. Are you willing to do it without complaining are giving excuses?

If so I want to work with you and show you how you can achieve your goals regardless of your current circumstances.

Are you ready? Let's do this together.

INSIDE THE BOOK

ABOUT THE BOOK

Next Level Voice Over Domination is a compilation of my first two books Steps to Voice Over Success and Voice Over Domination . The combination of these books with radical and amazing additional insights, is the most complete book on how anyone can build a successful voice over business. This book deals with not only what I teach, but how I teach, what I teach, why I teach it, and how you can learn directly from me. The book deals with my philosophy and the mindset needed to win in the voice-over business along with the step by step approaches with amazing tactics and strategies.. This is specifically for the voice-over artist that has a home studio and needs to understand how to start, build, and grow a successful voice over business.

Inside I discuss what it takes to win and then I go into some hard hitting tactics and strategies on your mindset to get you to where you want to be. I discuss your path and even how to take in-depth training with me so that I can help guide you and help you reach your goal of becoming a full time voice-over artist.

For in depth hard hitting strategies I would suggest going to my website. www.StepsToVoiceOverSuccess.com

"EARL HALL ROCKS! 1. He is generous 2. He obviously knows his stuff 3. He is committed to you doing your best 4. He has the guts to change & if I'm following in someone's footsteps I want to know that they are learning & growing. You must work with people who are walking their talk to get big results, I find."

Lindsay Wilson

World-Renowned MindValley Author & Mom Of Two

Chapter 1

YOUR GEAR

One of the biggest issues in voice over (there are so many) is what mic should I use? What DAW (digital audio workstation) is best? Should I use a Focusrite preamp or a PreSonus?

If you ask 5 different voice-over artists the same questions, you'll get as many different answers. This is one thing I can tell you. Your gear is personal. You develop a bound with it. It becomes a part of you.

For the new voice-over artist, these are major questions because you don't want to get the wrong thing. Here is the simple and real truth about buying gear.

You get what you pay for.

That is it. That is the real. When it comes to microphones. If you spend around $400-$800 dollars on a condenser microphone for your home studio, changes are you will never have to replace it.

That being said. If you are just starting out, a condenser microphone of about $150-$200 will get you going.

Check out my suggested gear at

https://www.amazon.com/shop/earlhallstudio

There are the industry standard mics that you see in most studios. The

Neumann TLM 103 and the Sennheiser MKH 416 shotgun microphone.

Those will run you about $1000, but will be all you ever need. Depending

on your recording space. We will get into your recording space later.

One of the questions I get all of the time is, "Can I use a USB

microphone?"

Actually, yes you can. The technology in some of the USB mics priced at

around $200 and above are amazing.

As you begin to get bigger and better jobs and more serious about your

recording space, you will want to invest in higher end gear. But to frank

you can build out a beginner studio for under $500 and it will last you for

years.

 The professional voice-over community uses pro gear and expect you as

person, even with a home studio, to use progear as well.

Check out my suggested gear a

https://www.amazon.com/shop/earlhallstudio

However, if this is a business that you want to build, let's just do this thing

right and start with the end in mind.

Get quality pro gear.

So, what gear will you need to start putting together your home studio.

Microphone $150-$400

Pre-Amp (i.e. Focusrite Solo) $100

Mic Stand (i.e. scissor mic boom) $30

Headphones $80

Pop filter $20

2 XLR cables $20

This is the basic setup you will need if you are serious about doing voice-over. The good thing about this is that there are not businesses that you can even start for under $1000. This one, voice-over, you can.

Later on in the book we will discuss one vital piece you must have. It's voice-over coaching.

Now, If you are intimidated by all this stuff. Don't worry. We all were LOL.

All of this gear may seem new and strange, but it will become second nature to you very quickly. Start looking on youtube for information on microphones, preamps, etc. There are some great folks to follow on youtube (besides me LOL) that can give you an amazing education on voice-over gear.

The Booth Junkie

Mike Russell

These two guys have amazing YouTube channels with tons of great

information. You can learn all about mics, preamps, and tons more.

"I can't say enough about the insights & personal, direct support I have received working with Earl in his Steps To Voice Over Success Program. I have learned so many new techniques for building my voice over business. These are cutting edge techniques - easily implemented methods that will continue to help me grow my business. It was easy to trust Earl's methods because they are the very same techniques that Earl employed as he grew his own business. He teaches what he knows - what has worked for him! Most importantly, his approach to teaching is highly professional & he delights in helping others to grow. Earl has given me the confidence to elevate my skills so that I can finally move from feeling like a part-time voice actor relying on "cattle call" auditions to building a professional brand that entices the high end clients I desire. "

Conchita Congo
Fulltime Voice Actor, Narrator & Copywriter

Chapter 2

MAKE A FIRM DECISION TO WIN

When I started doing voice-over in 2006, I "had no idea how to build a successful voice-over business". My skill set in voice over was at 0 and my knowledge of actually building a business in voice over was horrible. My integrity and drive was not enough.... it actually hurt the process of becoming successful because of the mountain of wrong information that was out there. **I was doing to much of the wrong things.** I was working harder and harder on the wrong path because of the wrong information.

Today, I am a go-to voice over business development expert for voice actors, podcasters, actors and even other voice over coaches as well. Voice Over talent all over the world get in line to learn from me through my YouTube Channel, Facebook group and of course personal one on one coaching. I teach a very powerful lesson on "**Stop waiting for permission from others to be grea**t. And the only way to reach your income goals as a voice over artist is to go after high-end clients." I have amazing strategies to teach with clients paying upwards of $10K to use his voice on their e-learning, commercial, and corporate narration projects.

"Wait a minute... How is that possible?", you might want to ask.

How did I go from "having no idea how to build a successful voice-over business" to becoming one of the most sought after voice-over experts?

How did I transform my mindset and realize that voice-over is not about being a commodity... but commanding high-end clients instead?

And how did I transition from being a broke voice-over artist to closing incredible deals close to $10k at a time?

I'll tell you what I did to change the game in just a second....

But first, here's what's most important for you to know:

It was not my intensity or my #grindanddontquit philosophy that kept me from being good at voice-over.

It was the fact that the sales and marketing methods I'd been taught were not even close to being relevant in today's market.

I have discovered that many of the most reputible voice over training companies are still teaching how to send postcards.

POSTCARDS! REALY?!

We live in a digital age and no one is rushing home to examine a postcard that they just got in the mail.

Those marketing and sales tactics were outdated and never yielded any results. They simply don't work anymore…. And they made everything inside of me scream "NO" **this is JUST NOT WORKING**.

Sound familiar?

See, I was basically left with 2 options:

Walk away from voice-over forever and give up because it just was not for me and I could not figure out the game.

Or…

Create a method that not only works with his intensity and #grindanddontquit philosophy, but that is built upon it instead using strategies that actually produces results

You've probably guessed it by now: I chose option 2 and I created my own voice over marketing and sales method - different from anything else you've ever seen.

A method that allows you to leverage your intensity, your work ethic, and the #grindanddontquit attitude and your desire to build a real voice-over business.

A method that's focused on smart work and connection with clients-with more clients being a pleasant side-effect of that.

And a method that's transformative, a method that actually works and that creates results beyond what you think is possible.

The one thing you can be certain of is this. If you apply the marketing and sales strategies within the Next Level Voice Over Domination mastermind (www.voiceoverdomination.com), you can go even farther

faster than I was able to do.

I'll never forget when I first started my voiceover business ... I knew nothing about how to find work or who to talk to. All of the VO coaches I called were recordings that said they didn't have time to speak to me. But one night, on a whim, I called Earl at 11pm, thinking that I would leave another message asking for help ... and the craziest thing happened; he actually picked up. From that moment, I have found Earl to be every bit as real as he says he is. I am so fortunate to have found him.
  -Anthony Pica

Chapter 3
Your DAW

So which DAW is actually the best? Well if you ask me then it is Adobe Audition. Why do I say that?

Because it is the one I know and have used the longest. It is as simple as that. Picking a DAW is like picking a brand of peanut butter. Whichever one you like is the one you buy. So many people stress out over it and really it just comes down to preference.

For me, Adobe Audition is the DAW that fits the voice over artist with a home studio the best. The functionality of it is second to none for ease of use and integration with plugins. My favorite plugins come from www.waves.com

That being said. The two most consider to be industry standard are Adobe Audition and ProTools.

There are many other brands to choose from. The one you learn on is usually the one you stick with.

- Adobe Audition

- Pro Tools

- Audacity (free)

- Garageband

- Reaper

- Studio One

The main thing you want to do is become a practitioner and expert of your DAW. There are pros and cons to anything, but the DAW you use is all about your productivity. In voice-over, the productivity factor is key. You have to be able to record, edit, process, and master your audio in an efficient manner. The first 6 months to a year is going to be your learning curve of whichever DAW you select.

Again, the most important thing is to dig in and become an expert at using it for voice-over. The great thing about what we do is that there is not a lot to really learn. Things like...

- Compression

- Equalization

- Limiting

- Normalization

- Gates

These are most of the key things you want to understand. Voice-over is much more than just sitting in front of your mic and recording your voice. Making your voice sound sweet with the help of your DAW is important.

Probably the best tip I can give in this area is...

LESS IS MORE!

New voice-over artists tend to over process their audio with too much compression and wrong EQ settings. In most DAWS there are indicators to let you know if you are too hot (loud). Green is good. Red is bad.

I have made an entire playlist on my youtube channel to help you with a bunch of this. Here is the link.

https://www.youtube.com/playlist?list=PLu0VuUfrsElAothjK_Ol3qbeer

S8lFTbj

You can also see my entire channel on YouTube at www.youtube.com/earlhallstudio

Your DAW is or will become an extension of you. Just like your microphone. If you are just starting, watch every video you can find on your DAW of choice. While you are watching, follow along in your DAW and do what you are seeing. Dig in and don't be afraid to mess up.

One of the first things you are going to want to do is watch a video on how to connect your gear to your DAW so that you can even record. This one part is where many get confused.

The good thing is that once you do this set up once you don't have to worry about it again, unless you change computers or DAW's

DAW's are very similar. If you understand one, then it is not that difficult to switch between them for the basic functionality.

"Super thrilled to have just accepted my largest book contract yet for a new novel called, "Son of Influence" by Erik Lewin. Made almost $1000 Over the last 2 days. Pretty awesome! Thank you Earl Hall as always for your training."

Anthony Pica
Professional Voice Actor & Audio Book Narrator

Chapter 4

DOUBLE YOUR SALES

If you doubled your ability to market and sell your voice over services, what's the change you could make in your life?

I want you to take a moment and really think about this.

How many more clients could you handle?

How would the lives of you family transform?

And how big of an impact could you make on your community?....

If you allowed yourself to overcome the fear and resistance toward marketing and sales and truly mastered this skill?

And most importantly: What is the loss if you DON'T learn how to shift your marketing and sales?

See, sales and marketing is not that hard. Anyone can learn how to grow a business....

Sales and marketing is about putting your gifts out there - and getting your skills to the people and businesses who need you the most.

And, obviously, this is important for anyone in business.... but it's absolutely crucial for you as a voice over artist.

Why?

Because you're not just selling a voice on a microphone. You're not just selling some "nice to have" accessories...

You're responsible for helping your clients grow their businesses. Think about that!

And the freedom, abundance, achievement, growth and success that come with it. So, as a voice-over artist, you KNOW how important it is to get your gifts out there - from you to the people and businesses who need you the most!

But I know….

That doesn't change your belief that you're "not good enough at voice over marketing and business development".

That you have no clue how to grow the voice-over business of your dreams.

And that selling and marketing is simply not your strong suit.

So here's what you need to know:

Marketing and Sales is not a talent. It's a learnable skill.

See, most VO's have a paralyzing misconception in their heads…that if they're not natural born businesspeople, they will never be good at marketing and sales.

But let me ask you this:

Are you a natural born voice-over artist?

A natural born expert in your field?

Or even a natural born audio expert?

Probably not.

And while sales (or online marketing) naturally come easier to some people due to their personalities and individual backgrounds, fact is that ALL of these things are learnable skills.

They can be taught. They can be practiced. And they can absolutely be mastered - by YOU.

You already have the skills and desire to perform on a high level.

You already know how to learn and execute on being a better voice actor.

And you're already committed to making a positive impact and changing the direction of your voice over business.

All you need?... Is a proven method, specifically designed for voice-over artists, that allows you to leverage these skills to create an amazing voice-over business.

So that you can serve at the highest level possible, help the businesses and people who need you (and are committed to creating excellence) and increase your own levels of abundance at the same time.

Which is exactly what I will teach you in Voice Over Domination.

Even with being unable to voice things for over a month now, it hasn't stopped me from getting my ducks in a row for marketing. I have a stack of jobs now to keep me busy until November because of what Earl has taught. They are just waiting! I feel like a #GrindAndDontQuit Evangelist!

-Thomas Machin

Chapter 5

YOUR RECORDING SPACE

You can own the best mic, the best preamp, the best DAW (if there is such a thing), but if your recording space is not set up right, none of that matters.

A decent recording space can make an inexpensive mic sound amazing. When I first started out in voice-over I was using an Electro-Voice RE20 with a Mackie mixer, a vocal strip, and two computers. I was recording in

my basement in a very pretty room. I thought I was doing it!

Do you notice anything a bit off in this picture (2008)? I had some amazing gear and thought that my voice-over production was top shelf. However, I was getting absolutely no work. Except for a $30 gig here and there.

Back then I had no clue that my entire setup was wrong. I obviously had the gear but...

MY RECORDING SPACE WAS CRAP!

When setting up a recording space you CAN NOT be surrounded by hard flat surfaces. This will kill the best audio. Hard flat surfaces allow your voice to bounce all over the room and back into your microphone. This causes your audio to have echo and basically sound awful. Back then I didn't know that. I actually thought I sounded amazing LOL.

There is a test that I created to check your recording space. It is kind of technical so you may want to highlight this LOL.

It is called the clap test. Stand in your recording space and...

CLAP.

If you hear the clap echo then it is not a good space to record. If you don't hear the clap echo, then you are good. It is as simple as that.

So how do you transform your recording space?

The secret is soft surfaces. This is a picture of me in my home studio in 2016, right after I purchased my Neumann TLM 103 (love the black version). You will notice here and in some of my earlier YouTube videos that I am surrounded by black comforters. Not walls! Even on my ceiling I have a comforter. During 2015 up until Oct 2017 when I moved into my

current studio in downtown Milwaukee, this is where the magic happened. In this simple setup I did voice over for major brands, documentaries, audiobooks, and regional radio commercials. I made a living right from my basement, surrounded by comforters, with my Neumann TLM 103 and Focusrite Solo. Oh, and my DBX 286s (the secret sauce).

NO!

You don't need a booth to get started or make good money.

Of course today I have professional booth and run an amazing audio

production studio :-)

Chapter 6

VOICE-OVER COACHING?

Yes.

I am amazed at myself (in the beginning) and with so many that want to get into voice-over that think this an easy way to make money. Now understand, in the first days of my voice-over career I thought that I could do all of this on my own. I mean everyone told me I had a great voice (have you heard that before).

I quickly learned that it takes more than just a good voice. One of the biggest hurdle to get over is to not sound like you are reading a script. The next is to sound natural.

Should be kinda simple huh?

Nope.

I am not sure what it is about all of this, but how do you sound like you are not reading and what do you mean, "sound natural?"

This comes down to what this all really is voice ACTING.

Being a voice-over artists is all about the acting. Having a good coach will show you the tips and tricks to accomplish this.

In finding a coach there are some things you need to be aware of. This is because different coaches can teach you different things.

If you are looking to learn how to do voice-over as far as delivery, script interpretation, and acting, there are coaches for that.

To find a good coach you can always ask other voice-over artists who they suggest. Just realize that finding a coach for this will come down to who you actually like. It goes along with the saying, "when the student is ready the teacher will appear." Just because another voice actor likes a certain coach does not mean that it will be a good fit for you and your personality. Finding a coach is not a one size fits all type of thing. Just realize you are in control of the person that you choose to learn from. A mentor is a very personal thing.

Then there are the coaches that can teach you audio production and how to use your specific DAW.

And finally, there is the coach that can teach you how to get clients. This coach is arguably the most important. You can have the best gear, the best delivery of a script, but if you don't know how to market and sell your service...

You are dead in the water.

When it comes to starting your journey to finding a coach or mentor, YouTube is a great place to start as well. Just search the term voice over coach and plethora of videos will come up. However, probably the best term to look up on YouTube is "How to build a voice over business". I mean that is what you really want to know, right?

Start watching and seeing the different coaches that are out there. You can watch their videos and see if their style speaks to your personally. You can also do searches on twitter and Instagram as well. Take your time with this process. Call up a few (that is if you can even find a number) or email them and try to start a dialog.

Pay attention to their response times and how willing they are to have a conversation with you. How someone treats you before you pay them is BIG indicator of how they will treat you after you pay them.

Having a coach and training a few times a year, even after you are established is a good idea. Just remember that the people at the top of their game get coaching throughout their careers to stay at the top.

- ▢ Michael Jordan

- ▢ Serena Williams

- ▢ Tiger Woods

- ▢ Michael Phelps

When I first got into the coaching arena, I simply gave out information for about a year before I started taking on clients. My claim to fame is showing voice over artists how to market. Because of the success of my students I am now a coach, the author of this book, and the administrator of a voice over facebook group with over 1K members called Steps To Voice Over Success.

We all have coaches and get coaching and mentoring through YouTube, blogs, books, and groups in Facebook and Linkedin. Look at all of these and when you are ready...

This bit here is from a blog I wrote.

There is a real difference between a voiceover coach and mentor. Both the mentor and the coach use the same set of skills but the differences between them are about the relationship.

In voice-over, there can be a need to have both a mentor and a coach. In fact, there may be a need or a desire to have more than just one. You could need a coach to show you how to deliver a script. Another coach to teach you how to do characters. Yet another coach to show you how to use your DAW and do audio processing.

Many of us have sought out a voice over coach. I mean, we hear all the time how we need to be coached in voiceover.

Is this true?

Now here is where for some of you I go left. However, for another set of new age voice-over artists, this is going to be gold!

First, let's take a look at what you need to be a voice over artists. It comes down to just a few things.

- Talent

- Technical Skill

- Above average marketing and sales ability

Talent is an easy one.

Either you have it or you don't. Sure, you can learn what you need to learn about how to interpret a script and voice inflections and transitions. Throw in some mic techniques and a little attitude when needed and you are about 95% there.

Talent is either innate or you must develop it. Either way, you need to practice and continue to learn and improve. I mean, Michael Jordan never stopped practicing no matter how great he was.

Technical skill

If there may be a roadblock, this is where it will be. I am known for saying that, "the home studio is the future."

By 2020 if you are not a competent audio engineer you will not be able to do voiceover. A decent voiceover with the ability to make their own demo and produce completely edited, processed, and mastered audio will the ones that get the work.

Think about this. Right now, we have the freelance sites, the p2p sites, and the agents. 20 years ago, it was all about having the right agent. By 2006 the p2p sites were all the rage and right along with them the freelance sites like fiverr, Upwork, and others became the promise for the voiceover artists.

What this did, however, was flood the industry with cheap, inexperienced voice over talent. Many of the people on these sites today really have no training, little talent, and use cheap non-pro equipment and gear. *(Please note I said many, not all).*

Let me pause here for a moment and say this. Many of the 'old guard' in voiceover are walking around butthurt because of what I just expressed about inexperienced voice over talent.

The truth of the matter is this. The voice over industry has changed and will continue to change. Just like in any other industry, you have to learn how to adjust or get run over.

No sense in complaining about competition. The radio can't complain about the TV. The TV can't complain about the smartphone or Netflix. You can not complain about the market. You adapt adjust and move on.

Things will always evolve and change. The market is the market. Pick your piece of it and stop complaining. It helps no one. Least of all YOU.

Sales and Marketing Ability

This is where the rubber meets the road. The voiceover artists that masters this will never be hungry. Your #1 Job as a voiceover is to GET CLIENTS.

PERIOD!

If you cannot get clients, I don't care how great you are in voiceover or audio production if you don't know how to market and sell your services, you lose.

Marketing and sales are the lifeblood of the voiceover. Not the agent, not the coach, not the mentor.

If there is going to be a decision in who to hire as a coach or a mentor in voiceover. Hire or align yourself with the one that not only shows you the craft of voiceover, but...

The one that can teach you sales and marketing.

Hint:

Many voice over coaches know nothing about sales and marketing in 2020. They are 10 to 20 years behind the times.

Look to the future of sales and marketing online. Look to the people on the cutting edge of Facebook marketing, Instagram marketing, email marketing, and yes Snapchat.

While you are sitting there saying that none of that will ever work. I just got another client.

"While on the phone today with Earl... I decided that I was going to boost a post. So I put a budget of 15$ for 3 days, 5 dollars a day. My post reached about 4000 people. Out of those 4000 people only one responded that wanted to work with me, but that one person ordered a 700$ job and has future jobs down the line. So that 15$ investment into the FB AD gave me a 4600% return. Now that should be a testament with what can be done."

Auston Kite
Professional Voice Actor

Chapter 7

DO YOU NEED AN AGENT?

So many people think that getting an agent will change their lives. The simple fact is that an agent gets you access to auditions. Not much different than what a P2P site does. In fact many agents use the same funnels to get auditions that the P2P sites do.

There are however many agents that may be in your local area that can get you on the local and statewide commercials that you hear on radio and see on TV.

To get an agent in some areas are better than others. I'm thinking now of places like L.A. and San Francisco. In those markets you usually have to be referred in by another VO before you can even get a phone call going.

However, in most other places you can simply call up a talent agency in your area and simply ask, "Are your accepting VO's on your roster?" It is really that simple. They will let you know if they are and what you need to provide to them in order to get on the roster. Once you are on their roster they will begin sending you auditions.

Even though I have 3 agents, they only represent about 5% of the work I get per year. 80% of my work comes from my only hustle and email marketing. The rest comes from the freelance sites that are out there.

Saying I have an agent can sound cool, but in the bigger picture they are simply one of my revenue streams.

Of course, to get an agent, you should have a great commercial demo and have gone through some voice over coaching as well. When looking for an agent you should also ask what kind of work they normally get. Like is it local, regional, or national. You want to also inquire of other voice actors already on the roster. Many times, you can see who they are right on the agent's website.

Chapter 8

THE METHOD

Building a voice-over business is tough. Heck, any business is tough to build. There is no lack of information out there on this topic, but an actual defined outcome, I mean literal results, seems to elude most.

In the voice-over community, there is no shortage of YouTube videos, blogs, or podcasts filled with information on how to build a voice over business. In fact, there are over 100 groups and pages on Facebook alone that claim to serve the voiceover artists (how many do you belong to?).

There is just one problem here. What are the outcomes being produced by any of them? Are you as a voice actor, not just being overwhelmed with information? But are you actually getting an outcome?

If you are honest with yourself, you are looking for the outcome of more clients and more money.

Why aren't you seeing this outcome?

Before you start blaming the information, the coach, or the Facebook Group, I want you to really start taking a look at yourself. We already established that there is no shortage of information. The problem, if you are still struggling, in many cases, comes done to your ability to execute on that information.

You bought the books

Went to the conferences

Watched the webinars

etc.

But nothing has changed for you? If I am sounding a little judgmental, sorry, not sorry. If this makes you a bit upset. Good. I want to at least try to shift your thinking here a bit.

When you are an entrepreneur, you are the only one you can blame. You are the one that started the business. You are the one building it.

Right?

The buck stops with you no matter what. You see with the access to all this information. With there being no middleman between you and getting clients (unless you let there be). With there being no barrier to entry and a completely level playing field, one thing is clear.

Either, you don't know how to build a business and/or your skills in voiceover just aren't good. Remember, you have all the information just like everyone else.

Even with all that only a small fraction of a fraction of voice-over artists will ever "make it". I know this all sounds a bit rough. I mean it to.

There is one simple fact. You will either make it or you won't. You will either commit to getting an outcome for your voice-over business of more clients and more money or you won't.

The method or secret sauce to all of this is you and your commitment to greatness. If you were looking to be handheld through a strategy. Sorry.

Earl Hall you are a gods gift to new voiceover artists such as myself. I would have been lost without all of the content that you provide. I can only speak for myself but because i am brand new to this business money is tight and with what you have shared in your knowledge has enabled me to be able to actually JUST DO IT. the more advanced courses which i will get there in time to work with you on a personal level will come. I can say that i personally have implemented A LOT of what you have shown. I am truly grateful. Thank you.

-Robert Caruso

Chapter 9

EMAIL MARKETING

Email marketing is hands down one of the best ways for you to build your voice-over business.

When I cracked this nutt it was the thing that made the biggest difference in my business.

The students in my course at www.stepstovoiceoversuccess.com have been crushing this strategy and realizing the benefits.

The strategy behind email marketing is simple

- Get a list
- Automate the process
- Reply to the responses
- Get the client

Ok, so let's break this down into actionable steps.

What I am about to show you is the actual strategy and tactics that I use to get new clients each and every month via email.

The important thing to remember with this strategy is this. What you do today will yield results 60-90 days from now. This is why it is important to do this each and every day. If you don't then you will not continue to get results.

In fact to make this book and the email marketing strategy even more valuable to you, here is a link to my full video training on it https://s3.ca-central-1.amazonaws.com/iirwebinar/free+webinar+bonus.pdf

I created this pdf file in 2017 to go along with a webinar that I did as a bonus. Now you have access to it as well.

The first part of this strategy is to get a list of potential clients. In the video training you now have access to how to use fiverr to get list of 1000 potential clients for as low as $40. Of course, you can build your own list from resources like google, Facebook, LinkedIn, etc. Buying a list can produce great results, but out of list of 1000 you will get about 2%-10% response rate. This is really good. All it takes is a few good hits to give you a client that could mean hundreds if not thousands of dollars to you each year.

The second part of the process is to put all of this on auto-pilot.

The best service I have found to day for this is www.mailshake.com

What Mail Shake does is allow you import a list (.csv), send out an initial email, and follow up emails according to a schedule. It uses smart technology so that if a lead responds to an email, they don't continue to get your follow-ups. If they never respond, then they will get as many follow-ups as you make.

This one thing alone is huge and when you see it in action you will be amazed. FYI, I make no money from recommending Mail Shake. I just know it has made the difference in my email marketing campaigns along with those of my students.

Right now, I want you to take full advantage of the training I am giving

you   access   to   at   https://s3.ca-central-

1.amazonaws.com/iirwebinar/free+webinar+bonus.pdf

Watch all of the videos and implement the strategies.

They WORK!

Chapter 10

Freelance Sites - P2P -

Social Media Marketing

These additional 3 opportunities can be a good portion of your revenue stream in voice-over.

Freelance Sites

There are more than a few these to choose from.

- Fiverr

- Upwork

- People Per Hour

- Freelancer

So many to choose from. An important part about working with these freelance sites is to know the rules. Also, know that they are all different. And most importantly, know that the people you do work for on these sites are NOT YOUR clients.

You are a service provider on these sites. In fact, you are not allowed to contact these people outside of the platform you connected with them on.

I have shared my own story before on how I was kicked off Upwork for agreeing to do work off of the platform with a connection I had made there (serious no no).

Here is a big part of the secret to using these freelance sites. Create as many gigs as you can for as many genres as you can.

One of the big mistakes I see people making is that they want to make one gig and put everything that they do into that one gig. What you must understand is that these freelance sites operate as somewhat of a search engine. If you do...

- Voiceover

- eLearning

- Radio commercials

- Radio imaging

- TV Commercials

- Documentaries

- Audiobooks

- Explainer videos

And whatever else you can think of, you want to create a separate gig for each specialty with the name of that specialty in the description and title of the gig.

You see when a buyer comes to a freelance site, they are looking for something specific. Not just voice over in general.

Another key point to make in working with these freelance sites is to price for what you are worth. On a site like fiverr , there is an idea that you should try and charge as close to $5 as possible.

Here is my thought. When a buyer comes to a freelance site they are looking for either the cheapest guy in the room or they are looking to spend money for quality.

You must decide which clientele you want to attract. If you are playing the pricing game, you will be a commodity and and always play the lowest price game. You will work yourself silly and frankly, you will come to hate it.

What I do instead is charge a rate that I am happy with. You see, when a quality buyer comes to a freelance site, they want to pay for quality. If you are only charging $5 then you automatically are not what they imagine quality is. Not to say that you don't produce quality. However, price dictates quality in the minds of many.

On these freelance sites your description and price will attract a certain type of buyer. So, why not attract the buyers that know quality comes with a nice price?

P2P

Pay2Play sites, in the beginning made everyone think that they could get rich just by signing up. In fact, they still do LOL. Since I am not going to talk favorably about the top 2 p2p sites I won't mention their names here. But... you know who they are LOL.

Some voice-over artists are making good money of P2P sites.

Some.

The clear majority of the half a million or more people on these sites looking for work are not getting it. Now to be fair. Many of the people on these sites are like I was back in 2008. Don't have a clue as to how to do voice-over.

I can't blame the P2P sites for the people on them that don't have the talent. However, you are probably one of the people that is probably not making a living just on P2P sites. If much at all.

Many of the people in the voiceover community are blaming the P2P sites for the declining revenue paid to voice-over artists.

Let me make this one statement here. The market is the market and they decide how much to pay. NOT the voiceover community. The market as well as voice-over is changing because of technology.

This is a good thing because there is no barrier to entry. No one can hold you back but you, your talent, and your ability to run an outstanding home studio. Those of us that understand the market and what they want will be the ones to win. Voiceover is not like it was back in the early 2000's.

Today with the right equipment and training you can run a very successful voice over business right in your own home.

All that being said. If you can make money on the P2P's then by all means...

DO IT!

Social Media Marketing

FaceBook (watching The Social Network now on TV. Go figure), Twitter, LinkedIn, Instagram, YouTube, and Snap Chat.

Should be on them?

YES!

Social media is just a slang term for the internet (thanks Gary Vaynerchuk). Knowing that you and all your potential clients are on social media is important. Please don't listen to the folks saying that social media is not important.

Many times, these networks are an easy into a client to make an introduction. The way in is to look at what your potential client is posting and adding value to the conversation.

I think it will be good here to say that building a voiceover business is a marathon, not a sprint. This takes time. In fact, if you are not willing to go hard on building this daily for the nest 3 to 5 years, then you can simply stop reading now.

Still reading?

OK.

Instagram is one the fastest growing social networks at the time I am writing this book. Facebook is the best place to be for marketing with ads and YouTube is the place to be to promote your expertise.

One of the little tips I got from watching Gary Vaynerchuk was all about promoting yourself on Instagram. He simply said. Do a search for hashtags (#) in your industry. For example. You could go to Instagram and search #explainervideo.

1. Look at the posts from all the different companies.

2. Follow them

3. Comment on their posts

4. Send them a DM (direct message) saying something like...

"Hey, you guys seem to make some great videos. If you ever need voiceover I would like to see if I can add some value to your final productions."

Literally sit down on a Saturday for 4-8 hours doing this (or until IG stops you from posting) and watch what happens. Spend a week doing this or months and imagine the connections and relationships you can build.

I did this over a period of a week and got 3 brand new clients just from that strategy from Gary Vaynerchuk.

Another great social network you need to exploit is LinkedIn. I mean you can do genre searches and literally find the contact person right there. As well as the links to their websites which will lead you to all of their social media pages.

Marketing is an activity that you must play with daily. If you don't, believe me, someone else will and they will win.

Chapter 11

Next Level Voice Over Domination

So What is Next Level Voice Over Domination?

It is the highest level mastermind available in voice over. The High-Converting Marketing and Sales System for Voice Over Artists Who Want to Work Hard and Get Results

Look, I want to be really honest with you:

Next Level Voice Over Domination is not just another voice-over coaching program that teaches you the old crap and tricks you can find in any corner of the internet.... Next Level Voice Over Domination is my life's work packaged into a program that's tailor made for voice-over artists like you - because it honors your work ethic, determination, and your integrity.

Yes, you'll get the exact strategies and scripts and you need to do better sales and marketing and get more clients.

Yes, you'll get the strategies, structure, and tested systems to replicate.

And yes, you'll easily double or triple your ability to sell and increase your income if you follow the steps provided in Next Level Voice Over Domination.

But what really matters is this:

Joining the mastermind Next Level Voice Over Domination will not only allow you to skyrocket your sales and your business.

It will allow you to create sustainable transformation in your business, to serve at the highest level possible and to get your gifts out there…. in a way that feels authentic and true and produces real results!

You must learn how to align with your purpose and serve at your highest level.

See, what I teach is radically different from any other voice over marketing method I've ever come across. There is no manipulation, no wasted time, and no reason why you can't win in his system... Just honesty, integrity and intensity - packaged into an easy-to-follow structure that simply gets you more clients.

When you align with your purpose, serve at your highest level, and realize your dreams you will discover even more is possible.

After all the training, after setting up your recording environment, mastering your DAW, and all the classes, now it is time to actually build your business. This is a lot of work but will pay you benefits for years to come.

I have said this before. You can learn strategy and tactics from anywhere. However, if that is true then why are you not where you want to be in your voice over business? **Something is missing right?**

You see, you don't need more information. You actually need transformation for your business. You need actual steps to take that can to get you to your goal. Beyond that you must overcome ALL of your self limiting beliefs. All of your demons holding you back.

You must begin to realize that you are enough. You are enough. You are enough. You can create your own reality and finally win.

Some of the things you must now learn will stretch you and sometimes even frustrate you. Depending on how strong your skill set is with technology, you will have more of a learning curve to master business development.

Business development has a few steps you must master

Marketing (some of these not all)

Facebook ads

LinkedIn ads

Social media

Cold calling

Email

Video Production

Blogging

Audio Podcasts

Sales

Landing pages

Funnels

Freelance Sites

Payment Platforms

etc.

One of the most important things you must master is yourself. Being aware of your talents, what you are good at, and what you need help with. Building your voice over business will rely on you as well as the people that you associate with that can help you.

Knowing yourself and mastering the negative talk in your own head will be an obstacle as well. Being able to continue on every day even when things are not looking the best is going to be key for you.

Patience over the next few months and years will be critical to your success.

This will not happen overnight.

Voice over is a very competitive industry. From beginner level to expert, there are thousands of people getting into this industry every day. The good news about that is that thousands leave the industry every day as well. This is because most people have no plan on how to start, build, and grow a successful voice-over business. They have no idea what it really takes to build a business. Having solid business development strategy is key. However, you must be flexible and willing to adapt to changing technologies and trends as they occur.

You must know what will work for you to be successful. One size does not fit all in this. You are unique and you must be able to see what your capabilities and talent will allow you to do.

For far too long we have listened to the 'so-called' voice over experts. Where has it gotten us? Are you still in the same spot you were in last year?

Low paying clients

No clients

Way less money than you need

If you are then we need to change that.

Let's get down to it and do what it takes to build your business.

You already know how to do voice over, so now you need to become firmly aware of how to do business development.

You don't need more voice coaching or lessons in producing a simple audio file.

You need to learn how to make money. You need a TRANSFORMATION not more information!

PERIOD!

Wouldn't you like to know..

The exact market you need to pursue

How to go after that market

How to get higher paying clients

The strategy you need to execute to make more money

This is what Steps To Voice Over Success is all about along with

Next Level Voice Over Domination.

Working with Earl Hall is like a dose of reality. He breaks down the business side of VO and how to get your voice in front of prospective clients. Besides knowing your craft, Earl drives home using strategies to measure what you're doing and to see if it's working. In summary, he challenges you to evaluate what works for you and discover what's holding you back.

-John Grimes

Chapter 12

THE FIVERR DEBATE

This is a quote from a person on one of my Facebook posts. He boasts about his podcast, audiobook deals, and how he came up from nothing to be a successful voiceover. He is very adamant about how freelancers that do work on Fiverr must be unprofessional.

This fiverr debate has gone on for years now. Many in the voiceover community have stated that...

People are keeping negative lists of freelancers that work on fiverr (never seen that list)

Freelancers on fiverr are beginners (but so many people on fiverr make 6 figures)

Freelancers on fiverr don't do good work (ever checked for freelancers on google and seen the same?).

You will not be respected if you do work on fiverr

All of this is complete nonsense. It's like every other place you could find a freelancer is an answer.

Let's be honest. You can come across a lot of freelancers on fiverr that will not be able to do the work you request. This is either because they may not have the skill, they may have bitten off more that they can chew, or the buyer made a bad selection to try and get off cheap.

Fiverr along with other freelance sites get a bad rap because of the price wars that go on. Freelancers bid against each other based on price (I NEVER do that and don't suggest it) and that can cause its own issues.

Sure we have people in each market that attempt to use price alone as a way to get business. They will do an enormous amount of work for $5. The truth is...

That is their right.   Freelance sites are a marketplace and we all compete the best way we can. If the only thing you have to offer is your work based on the lowest possible price, then that is a hard thing to sustain. Especially if what you do takes a lot of 'actual' work.

My main issue with all of this is this. Calling every person on any platform unprofessional is simply crazy. There are tons of great freelancers on Fiverr (along with a few that can make a bad name for the whole site).

What is simple frustrating...

Many people complaining about fiverr or making fun of it, have never even used, seen, or done work on fiverr.

If the bad talk about fiverr was actually true, please explain how I got a gig there from a major computer. One job, one client $6300.

That's all I have to say about that!

Lela Rhodes

"Work will always take you farther than talent. I hear your rant I feel your frustration. And I recognize your value. Thank you for working to make this world better even for the 1% who choose to participate."

Chapter 13

STOP F%$KING UP WITH SOCIAL MEDIA

Most of what I see voice over artists doing on social media is sharing demos. You share demos in voiceover groups on Facebook (won't get you clients). You share demos on Twitter (won't get you clients). No need to list the other social media clients. You do the same thing on those as well.

I also see voice actors promoting their services on these same channels and offering discounts. How is that working for you?

If you take a look at the posts that you have made over the past 12 months, how many of those have turned into actual work?

For most of you, probably none right? Well maybe for a few of you, you got 1 or 2 small clients, but nothing to write home about.

Am I right?

The main problem with this is approach is that you are going in for the ask on your first contact. In essence, you are doing the same thing as most other voice over talents.

I call it begging.

Well, there is a way to utilize social media that works.

The problem is that most voiceover artists do not have the patience to really work on this the way that it needs to work.

Instead of using social media to beg for work, how about using it in the way that benefits the potential client as opposed to YOU.

This approach takes a level of patience that most voice actors simply don't know about, or do not want to do.

As I go deeper into this explanation let me also say this. We have a tremendous amount of competition, not only from each other, but also from the freelance sites, agents, and pay to play sites that are out there.

From their perspective, they market to potential clients on social media by offering a solution to a problem. They pimp you out by offering high-quality voiceover for the lowest possible price.

We then compete with each other by lowering our prices further still. We compete, literally on price and then our talent, equipment, and expertise come last. In many cases.

To make things worse we like shiny new things. We watch webinars and videos selling us on the best new course for Fiverr or the best way to get clients on Craigslist.

We watch an ad on Facebook or YouTube from a coach promising you that you can get more clients and work if you just do 'this'.

Oddly enough, I am not faulting the coaches. Most of them do have real answers.

I'm faulting YOU.

You see, most people that want a full-time job in voice-over have no real talent when it comes to sales and marketing. Most are looking for what I call an 'easy button'.

That easy button mentality comes from laziness or simply not having a real business mind. For some reason, many people think that buying a microphone and learning Audacity makes them a voice actor.

It Doesn't.

Being a voice-over artist is more than your voice, your mic, or your DAW.

It is mostly about your ability to market and sell the service you provide.

It's a BUSINESS.

Marketing and sales, today is all about knowing how to use social media in the way that actually works.

Email

Facebook

Twitter

Instagram

SnapChat

LinkedIn

and others

are all valid ways to get business. That is if you approach it by giving your potential clients more value than the money you are looking to make.

THE CLIENT HAS TO BE FIRST NOT YOUR POCKET.

What I mean is this.

Instead of wasting time posting your demo in places that don't matter or begging for work in every Twitter post.

Try this.

What do you think would happen if you actually made a spreadsheet of your top 100 companies you really want to work with...

Discover how the decision maker is

Follow them on every social media platform they are on

See what they are actually talking about

Get involved in the conversation

Add value where you can

DM them about what you just read, watched, or viewed telling them how interesting you found it to be

AND DON'T ASK FOR THE SALE!

Again, DON'T ASK FOR THE SALE! Just talk to them about they are interested in.

Guess what will happen?

Over time they will do exactly what you want them to. THEY WILL LOOK AT YOUR PROFILE!

If you have developed a relationship with them based on their interests, the natural course of action for them is to find out more about what you do.

What will impress them more than anything is if you display a genuine interest in what they are all about. The fact that you resist the benefit to you and make it all about them will be amazing to them.

You will have taken the time to explore their interests and possibly even developed a good friend over time that is now in your corner.

Oh but wait.

This actually takes time, patience, and...

WORK.

In 2018, if you are willing to put in the time to do this, you could get several amazing clients willing to pay you your worth.

Or

You can continue to do what everyone else is doing.

If you work social media the way that actually works, you can change your voice-over career forever.

Thomas Machin

"It's not just new VO's that have made use of the boundless info you have available. I rewatch the videos and get something new."

Chapter 14

IF YOU SUCCEED IT'S YOUR FAULT. IF YOU FAIL IT'S YOUR FAULT

Over the past 3 years, I have heard this over and over again. Heck, I have even said it. There is this underlying attitude from new voice over artists and VO's that have been around awhile. The attitude is one of laziness on the part of the VO as well as ignorance of how to build a business.

When I first started in voice-over I looked for information online and in books in order to grow my voice over business. I even paid for courses. Not to mention the countless hours I spent, and still, do spend on YouTube and Google looking for information.

But why is it so prevalent that when a voice over coach charges for information that we get our panties all in a bunch?

We say things like...

It's a scam

They are taking advantage of us

Why do they charge so much

None of this is going to work

I have come to realize that those words are more a reflection of the voice over talent than the voice over coach.

I spent over a year just simply pumping out information to help the voice-over community. It was all free for the taking on YouTube. I even did free evaluations and training just to give back to the community.

The thing is you also have people out there like Bill Dewees, Marc Scott, Mike DelGaudio, Dave Courvoisier, Mike Russel, and many more that have done and still do the same thing. Give out information for free.

From YouTube videos, blogs, and podcasts, information is prevalent on how to build a voice over business.

There seems to be a problem however when these same people run a coaching 'business' as a part of what they do along with being a voice talent.

Why is this?

Why have we demonized these people for building a business that in any other industry it is considered normal?

Producing content on a regular basis is not easy. If you think it is, then please send me the link to your blog, youtube channel, podcast, or membership site so I can evaluate it.

Doing what these men and women do is not easy. And frankly, it is something that most people would not even attempt to do.

Of course, there are different styles, marketing strategies, pricing, and services that they all have for the voice over coaching business that they run.

Your challenge is to find the one that resonates with you and how you like to learn. That part is completely on you to make sure you do your research. That research is super easy. All you have to do is simply follow them, read their blogs, watch their videos, and decide if it is for you.

Here is the kicker though.

Before you sign up for a coaching program, you probably can find all the info on what you want to know already provided for free. Yep, they have already given it away.

Some people think that if they sign up for a coaching program that there will be some secret revealed that will change their voice over career tomorrow.

The fact is that if you are looking for an easy button, it doesn't exist. These men and women have spent years to develop their voice over businesses and there is no way you are going to duplicate their success without serious work over a few years.

YES, YEARS!

Building a voice over business is hard. Not many people will succeed. You will succeed if you change your mindset on coaching and looking for the information yourself. Believe me, the information is out there.

However, if you buy a course, pay for training, or research on your own, IMPLEMENTATION OVER TIME (YEARS) IS THE KEY.

Just imagine if you have hundreds or thousands of people emailing you, calling you, texting you, skyping you, IMing you daily asking you how to build what you have built.

Would you spend 20 - 60 hours every week doing that for free

Raleigh Harris

"I think of all the content I watch online, I watch Earl's stuff the most - including your website. I've actually decided to sign up for some of your courses/classes BECAUSE I trust you're expertise... you've proven that through everything you put out there. With others, it's a huge gamble. So I do appreciate what you've done for the VO community, and I say this as a newbie, but you've given me some of the "fire" you've shown in your vids/youtube/etc.. and for that, I'm grateful."

Chapter 15

MORE ABOUT NEXT LEVEL VOICE OVER DOMINATION

This is a high-end high results producing program that I created. The one outcome from this 12 month mastermind is to get you high-end clients. That is the one result that can be obtained in this mastermind.

One of the biggest issues that I address, right out of the gate, is mindset. So many people have a poor self-image or they simply just don't believe in themselves enough.

I realized long ago that many voice-over artists are simply not equipped with the ability to go beyond their own self limiting beliefs. This can center around issues with money. Not feeling good enough to charge an appropriate rate for what it is they do.

This can lead to competing on price (that will kill any business) on the multitude of freelance sites that are out there. Among many other things that block their ability to reach their income goals.

Trying to be the lowest cost provider for voice-over services will leave you broke, depressed, and can lead to you quitting the industry altogether.

I have outlined it here for you.

The Next Level Voice Over Domination Mastermind with Earl Hall is an exclusive 12 month mastermind completely focused on getting high-end clients in voice-over.

This is your opportunity to spend some one on one time with Earl Hall, over the next 12 months, to get you on track with building your voice over business and making more money.

Finally get a step by step strategy to build the voice over business you deserve.

What Do You Get?

- **Complete access to everything in Voice Over Domination. Close to 20 hours of training.**
  - Starting a VO Business
  - Using Audacity
  - Getting Clients on LinkedIn
  - Funneling Clients to you
  - Making more money on Fiverr
  - Advanced Training on ACX

- Business Development for Voice Over

- All paid webinars currently on the site

- BEST OF ALL you get all the training from my previous mastermind

Over the next 12 months you also get exclusive coaching on this.

Mindset

It is very true that information and access to it is not your problem. Execution is. More than that your mindset around your success and what you deserve in your business. In many cases, if your mindset does not change your business will never grow. The intention is to help you change what needs to be changed and build an amazing business.

Developing your marketing and funnels

Honing your marketing Outline also the start of the Copy for ads, freelance sites, and your website and Locking in your Mission Statement

Attracting Ideal Clients

How to communicate your true value

How to tap into your existing network (we give you the EXACT emails to send)

Registration and Landing Pages

Honing the Sales Funnel

Your Website and Freelance and P2P Sites

Closing the Sale

It is not about convincing people to buy from you. They should already be sold.

What to charge for your services

Follow Up - Sequences

Traffic / Refinement - How to use Facebook and LinkedIn Ads

- Developing your Facebook and LinkedIn ads

- Refining Your Ad Targeting

- Optimizing Your Funnel

- Website structure and copy

SUPPORT/FEEDBACK/FINE TUNING SUPPORT:

In addition to all of this, we have MASSIVE support:

2 exclusive training per month with me in our private Facebook

group- These calls are HANDS-ON! I can review landing pages,

Facebook campaigns, as well as answer any questions right on the

call. I'm there for marketing strategy, ad copy, and any mindset

problems.

You can also ask questions or submit anything you want critiqued to

us through the private Facebook group. We will review any copy,

landing pages, etc. and send you detailed feedback, or just help you

re-write.

I meet with you one-on-one for an hour each month to get Clear on your goals, set deadlines, and help you make the most out of your time in in the program, help you understand all resources and build a plan for success.

The Members-Only Facebook Group - You also have access to a private Facebook Group where you can get help from other program members, make friends, and celebrate victories!

In short, this is EVERYTHING you need to create a steady flow of high-paying clients that you love working with. If you can show up COACHABLE, RESOURCEFUL, and DECISIVE, and if you take MASSIVE ACTION, you will see a huge transformation in your business.

I'm really excited about working with you.

CHAPTER 16

YOUR NEXT STEP

Here is some truth for you...

You're a voice-over artist and you're not making enough money.

You've tried to make this work using freelance sites. You know them all.

You have all these rules to follow. You can even get banned or blocked at will from these sites for no apparent reason.

And worse, they don't even want you talking directly to the client.

The reason...

They aren't YOU clients They are theirs!

All you are is a service provider.

Now here's the real kicker. They try and make you compete on price!

You know what I mean.

You always have someone that is willing to do the job for less peanuts than you are.

Aren't you tired of that?

It's no wonder you can't meet your income goals!

How can you while you are racing to the bottom competing on price?

YOU CAN'T!

For far too long the information from all the gurus trying to tell you how to build a successful voice-over business has been wrong.

The information you've gotten from all the YouTube videos, podcasts, and blogs still has you confused and lost. You still have not been able to realize your dream of having an amazing business that gives you and your family the life you deserve.

Let's change that right now. In the next 24 hours, if you are really ready, you can get on the right path and off of the hamster wheel.

You've struggled long enough. I know that right before a huge breakthrough there is serious pain.

Well, you've been in pain, serious pain, long enough.

Now it's time for YOUR breakthrough.

If you are ready for your breakthrough, it would be my honor to help.

Go now to https://www.stepstovoiceoversuccess.com/p/one-on-one-with-earl

ABOUT THE AUTHOR

Earl is a sought-after voice-over business development coach who has a worldwide client base and has trained hundreds of others to market and sell their voice-over services - with integrity, honesty and determination.

His average income from just voice-over - for the past 2 years - has been over 6 figures. Whether you want to sell $99 quick VO gigs or $8,000 projects, his method is proven to create results - especially if you've been in voice-over more than 2 years.

Why? Because what he teaches is unlike any other marketing and sales method you've ever heard of for voice-over.

His approach is based on determination, integrity, truth and smart work, and allows you to leverage your VO skills and "sell" in a way that's authentic to you.

The skills that Earl teaches work everywhere, for everything and as he likes to say: "the only way to meet your income goals is to go after high-end clients."

How can you get more in depth training from Earl?

If you are a real beginner in voice-over. You can get **a free course** that will

explain what it take to get into voice-over.

https://www.stepstovoiceoversuccess.com/store/vCU8NPkq

For the highest level training there is only one thing that can actually work. This is the highest level training that provides the outcome of high-end clients. It is the Earl Hall Next Level Voice Over Domination Mastermind

It is by application only. It is for the voice-over artist that is ready to go to 6 figures or more. This 12 month long master mind is very exclusive and only available to those willing to honestly dig in and work.

It is completely focused on business development ONLY. So, you should already know the basics of voice-over and audio production. Get more information here.

https://www.stepstovoiceoversuccess.com/p/one-on-one-with-earl

Made in the USA
Middletown, DE
03 January 2019